Tokyo

Fun Kids Travel Guide

Table of

Tokyo	Introduction	5
	Japanese Food	6
	Getting Around	10
	Places to Eat	13
	Places to Stay	15
	Attractions	17

Contents

Activities Outside Tokyo	22
Geography	24
Holidays & Celebrations	26
Famous People	28
Etiquette	29
Final Facts	30

Introduction

Welcome to *Fun Kids Travel Guide: Tokyo*. In this book, you will learn where to eat, where to stay, what to do, how to get around, and other interesting facts about Tokyo. Enjoy learning about this fascinating and fun city!

Japanese Food

Popular Foods

Japan has many delicious and unique foods. Here are some favorites.

Tempura

Tempura is a Japanese dish of battered seafood or vegetables. This yummy dish is deep-fried, and the technique was taught by Portuguese living in Nagasaki in the 16th century. You can buy tempura at Japanese restaurants or supermarkets.

Gyoza

Gyozas are dumplings made from ground meat and vegetables wrapped in a thin dough. They can also contain ground pork, nira chives, green onion, cabbage, ginger, garlic, soy sauce and sesame oil. Gyoza shops however, often come up with other ideas for filling.

Curry

Japanese curry is one of the most popular dishes in Japan. People serve it with rice, curry udon, or curry bread. They also use curry sauce, vegetables and meat.

Ramen

Ramen is a Japanese noodle dish. The noodles are served in a meat or fish-based broth. The ramen is often topped with spring onions, sliced pork, soy or miso sauce, scallions, and other delicious ingredients. You can go to a ramen restaurant when visiting Japan to see what the dish tastes like.

Sushi

Sushi is a popular Japanese dish of rice in vinegar, sugar and salt. The main ingredients of sushi include seafood, vegetables and sometimes tropical fruits.

Sushi is often served with soy sauce, wasabi and pickled ginger.

Types of Sushi

Salmon

Ebi

Maguro

Ika

Hotate

Tamago

Amaebi

Unagi

Tako

Shimesaba

Ikura

Uni

Unusual Foods

In Japan, you can also find unusual foods and drinks.

Wasp Crackers

Wasp crackers are crackers with wasps in them. Wasps are added for flavoring and health benefits.

Elderly wasp hunters set traps in the countryside to catch the wasps. Next, the wasps get boiled in water and are added into the rice cracker mix.

You buy them in gourmet stores and markets.

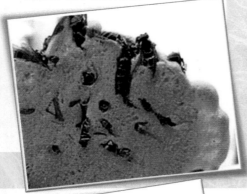

Fugu

Fugu is a Japanese pufferfish. The pufferfish is known to be notorious for the highly toxic poison -tetrodotoxin. Japanese people have been eating pufferfish for years, despite its potentially deadly poison.

The skin and the meat are both used in Japanese cooking and can be prepared in many ways.

Unusual Pop Flavors

During the summer, salty watermelon Pepsi is a very popular drink in Japan. You can also try mint cucumber flavored Pepsi.

Have fun trying these unusual options!

Getting Around Tokyo

The best way to get around Tokyo is to ride the Tokyo subway. It's easier than it looks.

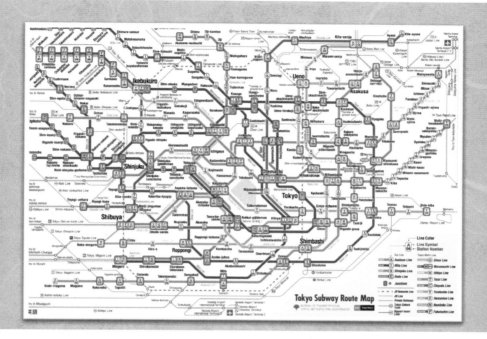

The subway has 13 lines with more than 250 stations! The trains have signs on the front telling you the destination, as well as announcements inside the train telling you the next station. Signs in the station let you know the name of the current station, and the next station.

A day pass costs about 600 yen, or you can buy a Suica or Pasmo card. Suica or Pasmo cards can be purchased online and picked up at the airport. Or purchase one from the ticket machines at the airport.

You will need to reload your card when it is low on balance. Reloading your card is easy because the ticket machines have English instructions.

Keep in Mind

- During rush hour, you are pushed into the train by transit staff. This way, lots of people can board the train.

- If you are staying in Japan for a while, getting single tickets is not a good choice.

- You tap your card in and out of stations and also if you need to change lines.

- For tickets, reloading, and buying cards, credit cards are not accepted.

Traveling Around Japan

Bullet Trains (shinkansens) are long distance trains that take you outside of Tokyo. Amazingly, these trains travel at 320km/h. That's 200mph.

The trains have a green car (first class car) and an ordinary car (economy class car). Most shinkansens have reserved and non-reserved seat carriages. If you don't reserve during peak periods, you may not get a seat and you may end up standing for the trip.

A ticket from Tokyo to Osaka costs 14,500 on the fastest train. If you plan on traveling a lot, consider getting a 7-day JR Rail Pass, which costs $US269 and gives you unlimited rides on JR trains, including most of the shinkansens (but not the fastest ones). You need to buy the JR Pass before you get to Japan.

Places to Eat

Japan has many cheap but good places to eat. Try out the restaurants mentioned below.

Convenience Stores

Convenience stores such as 7-ELEVEN and Lawson are everywhere in Japan. Japanese convenience stores sell a wide range of packaged foods that are really fresh and delicious. The sushi is awesome!

Also, your parent might want to know that 7-ELEVEN has ATMs that accept international cards.

Vending Machine Restaurants

Tokyo has restaurants with vending machines. You put your money in and then select what you want from the vending machine.

Once you have ordered, you wait for your food at a table. Pretty cool huh? If you pay more than the price, the machine gives you change.

Sushi Conveyor Belt Restaurants

Sushi conveyor belt restaurants are also common in Tokyo. You will be given miso soup and green tea.

You pick the dishes you like as they go past on the conveyor belt. Different sushi plates are different prices. A menu will say the cost for each plate. You can also order sushi from the menu.

Western Restaurants

If you need some familiar food, there are several North American chain restaurants in Tokyo. These include McDonalds, Burger King and Denny's.

They serve western food plus some Japanese options.

Where to Stay

Tokyo has many different types of hotels. There are normal hotels, capsule hotels, hostels, fancy expensive hotels, traditional hotels, etcetera.

Here are three interesting options.

Business Hotels

Business hotels, like Toyoko Inns, are a great choice when you are going to Tokyo. The hotel provides pajamas, toothbrush and toothpaste, and has a free breakfast. The hotels have non smoking rooms and have air conditioning in every room. Wi-Fi is free as well.

The free breakfast includes rice and miso soup unlike western hotels. You get a whole range of different foods. You can use chopsticks or cutlery.

Business hotels are similar to Western hotels, but the rooms are smaller.

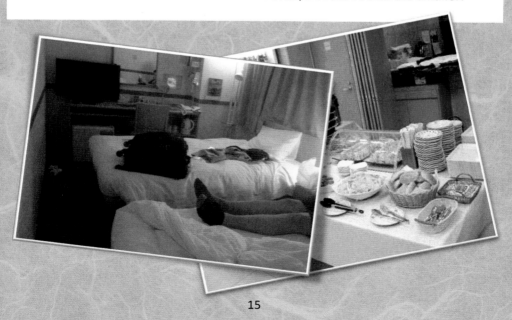

Capsule Hotels

If you prefer, you can stay in a capsule hotel, but do keep in mind that you are separated by gender and you have to be very quiet. There are individual showers and bathrooms at the hotel, as well as a locker to put belongings that you don't need, and a lounge for better posture on your electronics.

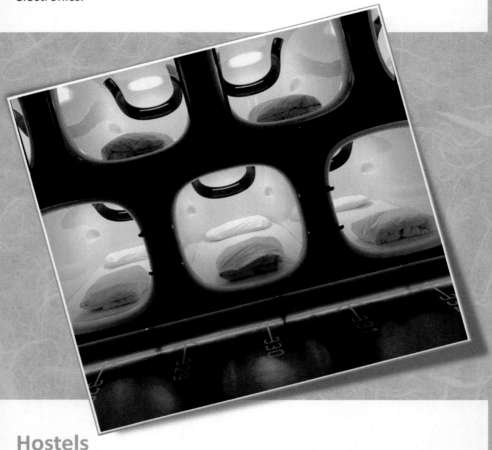

Hostels

A hostel is another place to stay if your family is coming to Tokyo. You may share a dormitory with people you don't know. The dorms have bunk beds with curtains.

Tourist Attractions

Tokyo has attractions to suit everybody. Check out these fun options.

Tokyo Sky Tree

Tokyo Sky Tree is 634 meters tall. It has a great view of Tokyo and sometimes Mt Fuji is visible.

There are lots of windows for viewing and even a see-through floor that you can stand on. You go up a really fast elevator to get to the viewing area.

Construction of this tall tower began on July 14, 2008. It is open from 8am to 10pm.

A combo ticket costs 1450 yen on weekdays, and 1550 yen on holidays for ages 6-11. The cost for ages 12-17 is 2350 yen on weekdays, and 2550 yen on holidays. Ages 18+ are 3100 yen on weekdays, and 3400 yen on holidays.

Tokyo Dome City

Tokyo Dome City is a theme park located at Tokyo Dome. If you have never been to this place, I suggest going. The park has a really cool roller coaster called the Thunder Dolphin. You can get skip passes if you go on a busy day. A one day passport is 4200 yen for people 18+ and 3400 yen for ages 60+ and 12-17.

Tokyo Edo Museum

The Tokyo Edo Museum is a famous historical museum which opened on the 28 of March in 1993. The museum has displays showing life in Edo - Edo was the previous name for Tokyo from 1603-1868. Opening hours: **9:30am-5:30pm**, but open until **7:30pm** on Saturday. Closed Monday, but open if Monday is a public holiday, in which case it is closed the next day.

Digital Art Museum

The Digital Art Museum is another recommendation. In the Art Museum, 3D art surrounds you with displays from forests, waterfalls, and other landscapes. There is even a tea house called the En Tea house. It serves tea with a 3D effect. Plants and flowers grow in your tea. The museum will amaze you.

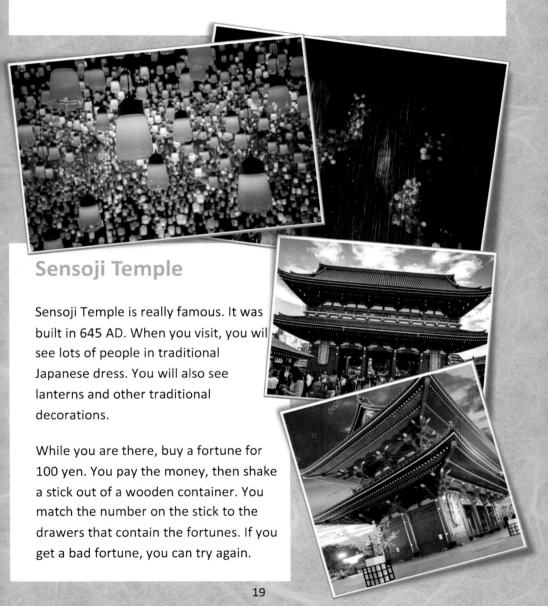

Sensoji Temple

Sensoji Temple is really famous. It was built in 645 AD. When you visit, you will see lots of people in traditional Japanese dress. You will also see lanterns and other traditional decorations.

While you are there, buy a fortune for 100 yen. You pay the money, then shake a stick out of a wooden container. You match the number on the stick to the drawers that contain the fortunes. If you get a bad fortune, you can try again.

Joypolis

Joypolis is an indoor theme park located in Tokyo. Opened on July 20, 1994, Joypolis is very well known for the rides. The park also has a lot of games to play. The location is DECKS Tokyo beach. Opening hours are from 10am to 10pm.

Meiji Shrine

Meiji Shrine is one of the must-do attractions in Tokyo. You first walk through Yoyogi Park to get to the Shrine. At the Shrine, you do the ritual of washing your hands. You will find out how to do this when you are there.

You can also make an offering (bow twice, clap twice, say a prayer, clap once more) or buy fortunes for good health, long life and other things. The park is easy to get to by subway.

Toyota Mega Web

Toyota Mega Web is another exciting destination. Check out the cool cars and try the awesome driving simulators. The Mega Web is very close to the Digital Art Museum.

National Museum of Emerging Science and Innovation Miraikan

This museum is a very fun place to go. There are many interactive exhibits including a very cool internet simulation.

You can see a demonstration of Asimo the robot or ride on a UNI-CUB, which is like a small Segway.

Opened on July 9, 2001, this museum was created by Japan's Science and Technology Agency.

Out of Tokyo

Heading out of Tokyo? Here are some fun ideas.

Snow Monkey Park

At the Snow Monkey Park you get to experience snow monkeys wandering right by you. During the winter the snow monkeys hang out in the hot springs.

There are strict rules on food because the monkeys grab the food from you! You can do tours or find your own way using the easy-to-use train and bus system.

Kubiki Trail

The Kubiki trail is a cycling trail located next to the Sea of Japan. It used to be a train line, so there are some fun tunnels to ride through.

You can rent electric assist or regular bikes from the shinkansen station. The park has a map so you know where you want to ride, along with a convenience store.

Part way along the trail, there is an area known for snow crab and you can get delicious crab snacks.

Nagoya Train Museum

Located in Nagoya is an excellent train museum. The museum has train models to look at and you can even go inside many of them. Make sure to try the maglev simulation and the shinkansen driver simulation. The huge diorama of model trains is good, too.

Noodle Cup Museum

The Noodle Cup museum is in Yokohama, Japan. You learn about the history of ramen, which is interesting. You can also explore different containers of ramen and when they were invented.

Don't forget to sign up to design a ramen cup and also to make ramen. The ramen-making takes about half an hour and you get to take the noodles home.

Geography of Japan

Japan is a country made up of thousands of islands. The four main islands are Honshu, Kyushu, Hokkaido and Shikoku. Japan's size is about the same as California or Germany.

Japan's closest neighbors are North & South Korea, China and Russia.

Because the country extends a long way north-south, the climate is quite different in Hokkaido and Kyushu.

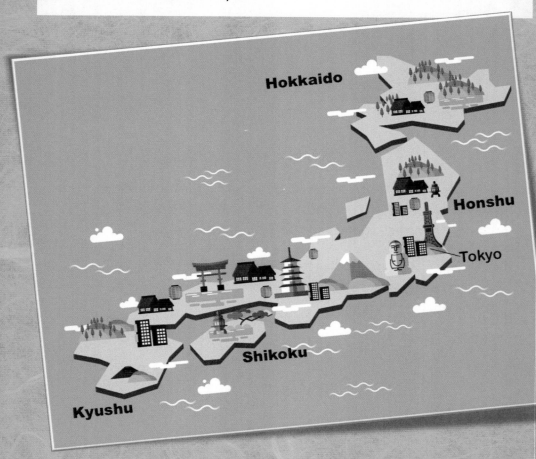

Over 70% of Japan's terrain is mountainous. Because it is located on the ring of fire, Japan has many volcanoes as well.

Mt Fuji

The most famous volcano in Japan is Mt Fuji. It is the tallest volcano in Japan at 3776m.

Sometimes you can see Mt Fuji from high points in Tokyo, or from the bullet train (shinkansen) as you travel from Tokyo to Nagoya.

Earthquakes

Because Japan is on the Pacific Ring of Fire (a place where tectonic plates merge), it has a lot of earthquakes. You might feel a small one while you are there.

Holiday & Celebrations

Japan has many holidays and celebrations. Here are some of the most well-known ones.

Golden Week

Late April/Early May

Golden Week is a collection of four public holidays within seven days. Many people take a whole week off so make sure to make reservations for hotels and trains if you are traveling during this busy week.

Hina Matsuri (Doll's Festival)

March 3

On this day, families with girls pray for their health and happiness.

Children's Day

May 5 (Part of Golden Week)

This day celebrates children and families. Families hang up koi kites.

Sticky rice cakes are a traditional food served on this day.

Emperor's Birthday

February 23

On the Emperor's birthday, a public ceremony takes place at the Imperial Palace in Tokyo.

The gates of the palace are opened to the public and the Emperor and Empress appear on a balcony to acknowledge the crowd.

This holiday is held on Emperor Naruhito's actual birthday. The date changes when there is a new emperor. Because Emperor Akihito abdicated in 2019, 2020 Is the first year to have the holiday on February 23.

Famous People

Everyone will be impressed if you can talk about these three famous Japanese people.

Basho

Basho was a famous haiku writer who was born in 1644 and died in 1694. Haikus are a poem with a 5 syllable line, then a 7 syllable line, then another 5 syllable line. Basho wrote a lot of haikus in his life. His birthplace is Iga Province.

The Emperor of Japan

Naruhito is the Emperor of Japan. His birthday is February 23, 1960. Naruhito has been on the Chrysanthemum Throne since his father Akihito abdicated in 2019.

Hokusai

Hokusai was a famous Japanese artist. He was born on October 31, 1760 in Edo (the old name for Tokyo) and died on May 10, 1849. This tsunami picture is his most famous work.

Etiquette

Here are some ways that Japan might be different from your country.

Eating in Public

In Japan, eating while walking in public is considered very impolite. Instead, wait until you get back to where you are staying. Or sit down in a seating area as an alternative. Find the nearest seat quickly if you order something like ice-cream, because it can obviously melt.

Pouring Your Own Drink

If you are in Japan, never pour your own drink. You pour the drink for your partner and your partner pours it for you. Like with eating in public, it is considered very impolite to pour a drink for yourself.

Toilet Slippers

In Japan, you may come across bathroom slippers. You wear them in the bathroom only to ensure that dirt is not spread to other parts of the house. Toilet slippers are worn in a many homes and even some restaurants/businesses.

Final Facts

You are now ready to enjoy your trip to Tokyo! Here are some final facts to make you an expert on this awesome city.

Population

Japan: 126.8 million

Tokyo: 9.3 million

Handy Phrases

Hello: Kon-ni-chi-wa

Please: ku-da-sa-i

Thank you: A-ri-ga-to

Flag

Weather

Spring: Mild days, chilly evenings

Summer: Hot with high humidity

Fall: Warm with cool evenings

Winter: Cold and sunny

Enjoy your
trip to Japan!

Acknowledgements

Photos used with thanks from the following sources:

Unsplash.com

Pixabay.com

DepositPhotos.com

Private collection of BJ

Design Help

Thanks to B Wilson & J Toole

About the Author

B Jenkins is a fun teen who loves to travel. When he's not in school, he likes swimming, skiing and screen time.

Made in the USA
Coppell, TX
03 June 2024

33054126R00021